Backyard Animals
Skunks

Annalise Bekkering

Weigl Publishers Inc.

Published by Weigl Publishers Inc.
350 5th Avenue, Suite 3304, PMB 6G
New York, NY 10118-0069
Website: www.weigl.com

Library of Congress Cataloging-in-Publication Data

Bekkering, Annalise.
  Skunks / Annalise Bekkering.
      p. cm. -- (Backyard animals)
  Includes index.
  ISBN 978-1-59036-685-1 (hard cover : alk. paper) -- ISBN 978-1-59036-686-8 (soft
cover : alk. paper)
  1. Skunks--Juvenile literature. I. Title.

QL737.C248B45 2008
599.76'8--dc22

                                                                    2006102111

Printed in the United States of America
1 2 3 4 5 6 7 8 9 0 11 10 09 08 07

Editor Heather C. Hudak
Design and Layout Terry Paulhus

Cover: Some people call skunks stink cats or smell cats.

All of the Internet URLs given in the book were valid at the time of publication. However,
due to the dynamic nature of the Internet, some addresses may have changed, or sites may
have ceased to exist since publication. While the author and publisher regret any
inconvenience this may cause readers, no responsibility for any such changes can be
accepted by either the author or the publisher.

Every reasonable effort has been made to trace ownership and to obtain permission to
reprint copyright material. The publishers would be pleased to have any errors or omissions
brought to their attention so that they may be corrected in subsequent printings.

Contents

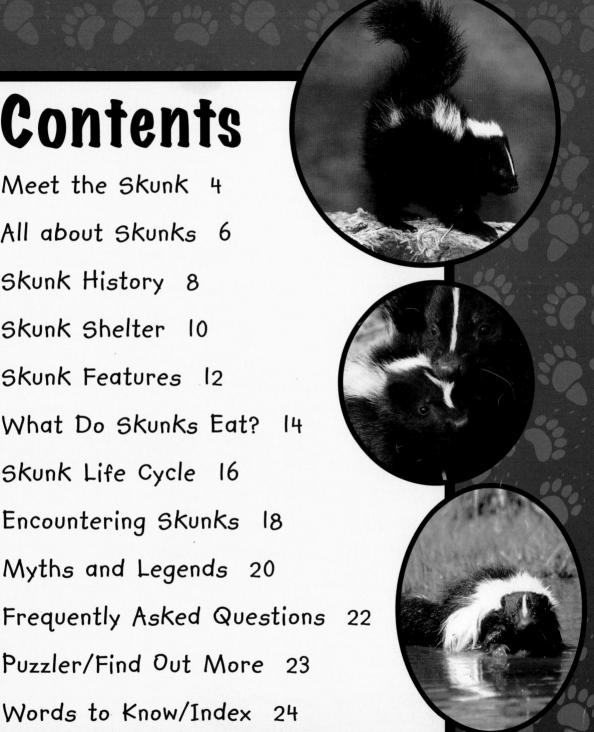

Meet the Skunk

Skunks are **mammals**. They have long, black and white fur with stripes, swirls, or dots. A skunk has a small head, small ears, short legs, and a long, fluffy tail. It is about the same size as a house cat.

Skunks are shy, clean animals. They are not aggressive. This means they will run away rather than fight. When a skunk is angry or scared, it will stamp its feet and growl or hiss.

Skunks protect themselves with their scent, or musk. When a skunk feels threatened, it warns its enemies by standing on its front legs. If its enemies do not run away, the skunk sprays them with a stinky spray. A skunk can spray up to 10 feet (3 meters). This odor is hard to wash off, and it can last many days.

The smell of a skunk's spray can carry on the wind for up to 1 mile (1.6 kilometers).

A skunk has only a small amount of spray. It will not use its spray without first warning the other animal.

All about Skunks

There are many skunk **species** in North and South America. They include spotted skunks, hog-nosed skunks, hooded skunks, and striped skunks. All wild skunks are black and white, and they have a stinky spray.

Skunks are related to two species of stink badgers. Stink badgers live in Indonesia and the Philippines. Each type of skunk is different in appearance and behavior.

The most common skunk in North America is the striped skunk. The body of a striped skunk forms a "U" shape when the animal sprays an enemy.

Colors of Skunks

Hog-nosed Skunks

- Most hog-nosed skunks have a white tail and a single white stripe along their back.

Hooded and Striped Skunks

- The striped skunk has two large white stripes from head to tail, which meet at the head.
- The hooded skunk has a white back or black back, with white stripes along its side.

Spotted Skunks

- The eastern spotted skunk has one white spot on its forehead and dotted lines along its back, with a black-tipped tail.
- The western spotted skunk has thick, broken, white stripes on its back, with a white-tipped tail and a white spot between its eyes.

Skunk History

Skunks are native to North and South America. Some American Indian groups kept skunks as pets. Farmers used skunks to hunt pests, such as rodents.

For many years, skunks were trapped for their fur. Skunk fur was used to make coats and jackets. In the 1950s, skunk fur became less common for clothing. Today, skunks are rarely trapped for their fur.

Skunk musk is used in some perfumes. First, the smelly odor is removed. Then, it is used as the base of the perfume. This helps the scent to stay on the skin for a long time.

Skunk cabbage is a wildflower that smells like a skunk.

Some skunks use their musk to scare away enemies.

Skunk Shelter

Skunks can be found in fields, forests, and grasslands. Some live in towns and cities. Skunks live in dens that they dig themselves or in those abandoned, or left empty, by other animals. Skunks may live in tree stumps, woodpiles, and under decks or buildings.

A skunk's den can have many entrances. The animal lines one chamber in the den with leaves and grasses. This nest is used to sleep in and to raise young.

Skunks plug the entrance of the den with leaves and grasses to protect themselves from the cold. In winter, skunks only come out of their den on warm days.

Fascinating Facts

In winter, male skunks leave the den to search for food. Females stay inside the den.

Most skunks live within 2 miles (3.2 km) of water.

Skunk Features

A skunk's body is **adapted** to protect it from **predators**. Skunks have many predators, such as coyotes, foxes, cougars, owls, and **domestic** dogs. An animal that is sprayed by a skunk will learn to avoid hunting animals that are black and white.

EYES
Skunks cannot see well. They must rely on their sense of smell to find food.

SHARP CLAWS
Skunks use their long, sharp claws for digging in the dirt and searching for food. Skunks eat grubs and worms that they dig out of the ground or rotting wood.

SCENT GLANDS

Scent **glands** under a skunk's tail make a thick, yellow, oily spray. The glands are the size of a grape. They hold enough musk for about five or six sprays. A skunk's spray can make a person ill. It can make the eyes burn, so the person or animal cannot see for a short time.

LEGS

A skunk's legs are short, so they move slowly. Skunks waddle when they walk. Most cannot climb fences or trees because of their short legs.

What Do Skunks Eat?

Skunks are omnivores. This means that they eat both meat and plants. Skunks eat insects, mice, fish, fruit, nuts, and leaves. Some skunks eat bird and turtle eggs.

In spring and summer, skunks mostly eat worms and insects, such as grasshoppers, crickets, wasps, and bees. In autumn and winter, skunks eat equal amounts of animals and plants.

Skunks are nocturnal. Nocturnal animals are more active at night than during the day. Skunks begin searching for food after sunset. They search for food near their den.

Skunks roll caterpillars around on the ground before they eat them. This removes the caterpillars' hair and makes them easier to eat.

Skunks sometimes eat garbage, birdseed, and pet food.

Skunk Life Cycle

Female skunks begin mating when they are one year old. Most skunks mate in February or March. Baby skunks, called kits, are born in May.

Newborn

When a skunk is born, it weighs about 0.5 ounce (14 grams). Kits are nearly hairless at birth. Kits are covered with hair by 13 days old. At 2 to 3 weeks, their eyes open. Kits leave the den with their mother when they are 7 weeks old.

2 to 6 Months

Kits drink their mother's milk until they are 2 months old. They stay with their mother until autumn. Some kits stay in their mother's den throughout the winter.

Most skunks have one **litter** per year. There can be one to ten kits in a litter. The female skunk raises the litter of kits by herself. Female skunks are very protective of their kits. The mother skunk will spray predators.

Adult

Most adult skunks live alone. During cold weather, females may live in the same den. In nature, most skunks live for about 3 years.

Encountering Skunks

Skunks like to eat honey and bees. They may eat chickens from farms. Skunks sometimes dig up gardens looking for grubs and worms. They raid garbage cans for kitchen scraps. Skunks also hunt mice.

Most skunks are shy. If they act aggressively, they might have **rabies**. Skunks can carry ticks, fleas, ringworm, and lice.

People should not approach a skunk in nature. It is best to move away slowly so the skunk does not become scared and spray. An orphaned or injured skunk may need special care. Call a veterinarian for help.

Useful Websites

To learn more about skunks, visit
http://dnr.wi.gov/org/caer/ce/eek
Type the word "skunk" into
the search field.

Great horned owls are predators of skunks. Great horned owls do not have a good sense of smell. They are not affected by a skunk's spray.

Myths and Legends

There are many American Indian legends about skunks. Some of the legends tell how the skunk got its stripes. Others tell about its smell.

In one legend, the skunk is a trickster. He outwits Coyote. Skunk and Coyote race to see who will enjoy a meal of prairie dog meat that is cooking on a fire. Coyote gives Skunk a head start, but he soon passes by. Coyote does not notice Skunk hiding in a patch of grass. Skunk does not complete the race. Instead, he turns back to take the meat from the fire.

The city of Chicago's name may come from an Ojibwa Indian word that means "the place of the skunk."

The First Skunk

*This Winnebago Indian legend is about a **vain** girl who learns a lesson about inner beauty.*

There was once a baby girl born with pure white hair. The girl grew up to be very beautiful. She was very vain. The girl would spend many hours staring at herself in the water.

One day, a man wanted to court the girl. The girl thought he was ugly. The man was Turtle. Turtle was one of the great spirits. He wore a disguise. Turtle shed his skin and became beautiful. Turtle told the young woman, "Since you reject me, I will change you into a common animal. When people see you, they will look away because of your terrible odor."

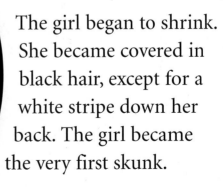

The girl began to shrink. She became covered in black hair, except for a white stripe down her back. The girl became the very first skunk.

Frequently Asked Questions

How do I know if I have skunks in my yard?

Answer: One sign of skunks is a strong, stinky, musky smell in the air. You might see droppings, tracks, and holes dug in the ground.

How can I keep my cat or dog from being sprayed by a skunk?

Answer: Keep your pet inside at night. This is when skunks are most active. Fit tight lids on your garbage, and do not put your pet's food outside.

How do skunks find insects?

Answer: Skunks will dig in the ground for insects. The holes they leave are about 1 to 2 inches (2.5 to 5 cm) deep and 3 to 4 inches (7.6 to 10 cm) wide.

Puzzler

See if you can answer these questions about skunks.

1. Name four species of skunks.
2. Where is a skunk's spray made?
3. What are skunks' main predators?
4. How many kits are in a litter?
5. How long do skunks live in nature?

Answers: 1. spotted, hog-nosed, hooded, and striped 2. in glands under the tail 3. great horned owls 4. one to ten 5. about 3 years

Find Out More

Skunks are exciting animals, and there are many more interesting facts to learn about them. Look for these and other books about skunks at your library.

Mason, Adrienne. *Skunks*. Kids Can Press, 2006.

Swanson, Diane. *Welcome to the World of Skunks*. Whitecap Books, 1999.

Words to Know

adapted: adjusted to the natural environment

domestic: an animal that has been trained to live with people

glands: in skunks, a group of cells that produce a stinky spray

litter: several babies born at one time to the same mother

mammals: animals that have fur, make milk, and are born live

predators: animals that hunt other animals for food

rabies: a disease caused by a virus that can be spread from animals to humans and other animals

species: animals or plants that share certain features

vain: thinking highly of oneself

Index